Dedicated to Elena and Norma Olivi

ABIDE WITH ME

Sw. : Oboe, Tremulant
Ch. : Strings
Gt. : Flute 4′, Tremulant
Ped. : 16′ 8′ Ch. to Ped.

EVENTIDE
William H. Monk
Arranged by Diane Bish

add Ch. 16' 4' Couplers
add Ch. to Ch. 4'16'
With more movement
add Bourdon 16'
add Bourdon 32'
Bourdon 16' 32' off

Gt.
Ch. to Ch. 16' 4' off
Sw. Oboe
Ch.
reduce stops
ppp

Dedicated to Mollie Weaver

IN THEE IS GLADNESS

Sw. : Flute 8′ 4′ 2′, small mix.
Pos.(Ch.) : Flute 8′1′
Ant. : Flute 8′ 2′
Gt. : Principals 8′ 4′ 2′, **mix.**
Ped. : Soft 16′ 8′, Ch. to Ped.

J.S. Bach
Arranged by Diane Bish

Joyful, detaché

a tempo
mp

detaché
Sw.
mf
8′, 4′, 2 2/3′
simile
Ch. Clarinet

Anti.
Gt. Fond. 8′, 4′, 2′ mix

rit.
a tempo
ff
mp
Anti.
Sw.
Gt.
f

Sw. solo Trumpet
Gt.

ff
Anti.
Sw.
Gt.
Anti.
Pos.

As beginning
detaché
mp Flutes 8′, 1′
simile

f
Broaden
ff
a tempo
mp

Dedicated to Daniel Miller

MORNING HAS BROKEN

Sw. : Oboe, Tremulant
Ch. : Erzahler, String celeste
Gt. : Flute 4′, Tremulant
Ped. : Soft 16′, Ch. to Ped.

BUNESSAN
Traditional Gaelic Melody
Arranged by Diane Bish

Andante-very smoothly

Oboe
– Oboe
Gt. prime
cresc. gradually
+ Sw. reeds 16′, 8′, 4′

Solo Tr.

Ch.
sim.
– Sw. reeds

8
sim.
cresc.
Gt.
+Sw. reeds
Gt.

rit.
a tempo
rit.

Dedicated to Beverly Atkinson

THIS IS MY FATHER'S WORLD

Sw. : Oboe, Tremulant
Ch. : Strings
Gt. : Flutes 8′ 4′, Principal 8′
Ped. : Soft 16′, Ch. to Ped.

TERRA BEATA
English Melody
Arranged by Diane Bish

Gt.
Oboe
Ch.

Ch.
Gt. + 4′ Fl. only
+ Ch. to Ch. 4′
sim.

tr
Ch.
cresc.
—Ch. to Ch. 4′
Fl. 4′

pp
pp
Gt.
gradual cresc. and accel.
+ Sw. 16′, 8′, 4′ reeds
Marcato-strong rhythm
f

ff

Dedicated to Richard Parks

WHEN I SURVEY THE WONDROUS CROSS

Sw. : Strings
Ch. : Clarinet, Tremulant
Gt. : Principals 8′ 4′ 2′
Ped. : Soft 16′, Sw. to Ped.

HAMBURG
Based on Gregorian Chant
Arranged by Diane Bish

+ Sw. to Sw. 16′, 4′
3
3
+32′ untersatz
+ Flutes 8′, 4′

*Do not repeat melody notes

+ Strings 8′, 4′

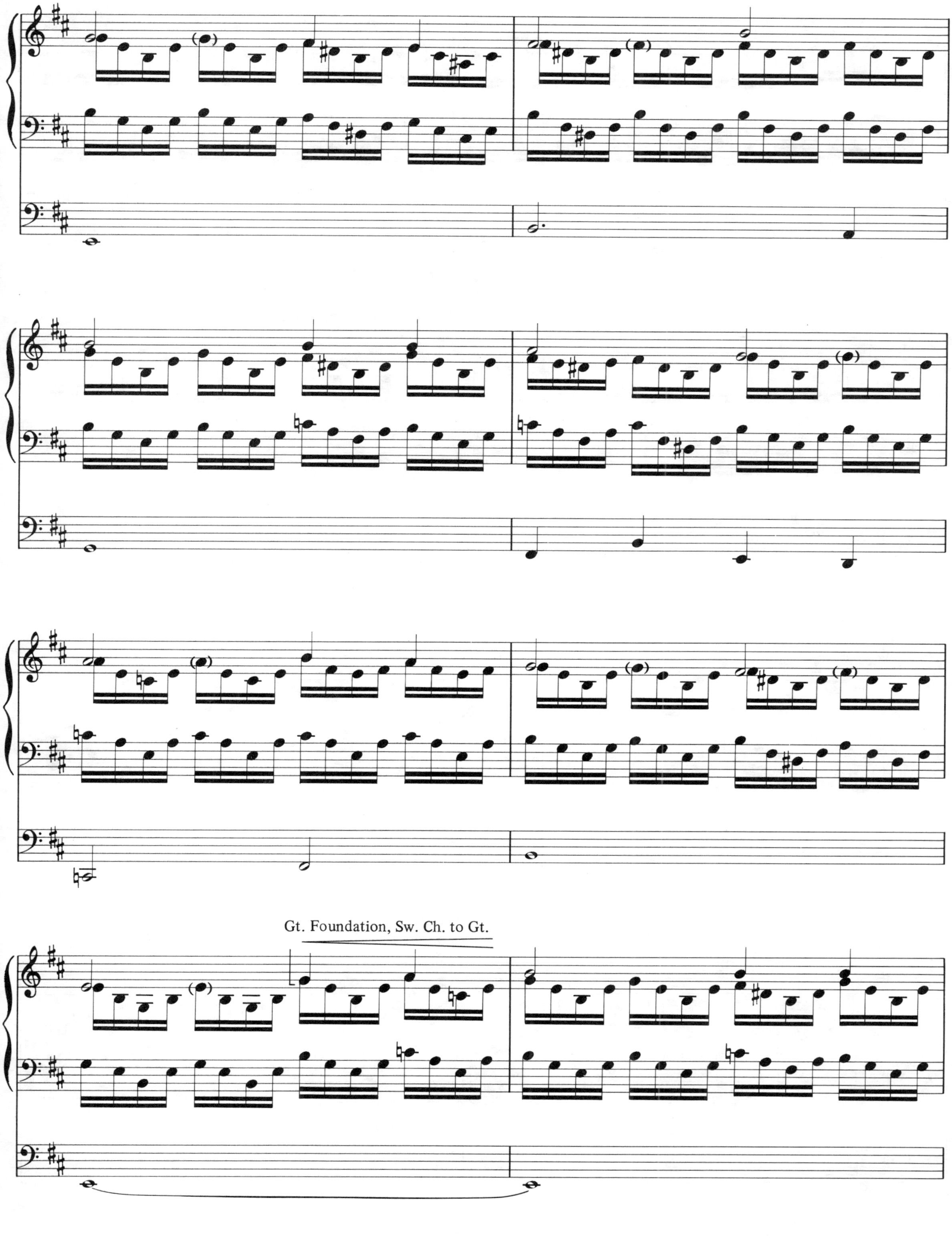
Gt. Foundation, Sw. Ch. to Gt.

gradual cresc.
rit.
A tempo-more briskly
Full with mix
ff
cresc.
to end
+32′

+ Sw. 16′ 8′, 4′ reeds
+ 4′ coup to Gt.

Broaden
a tempo
rit.
fff
fff